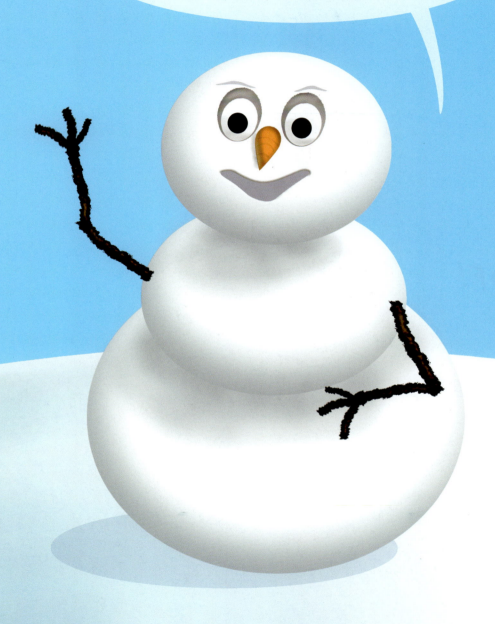

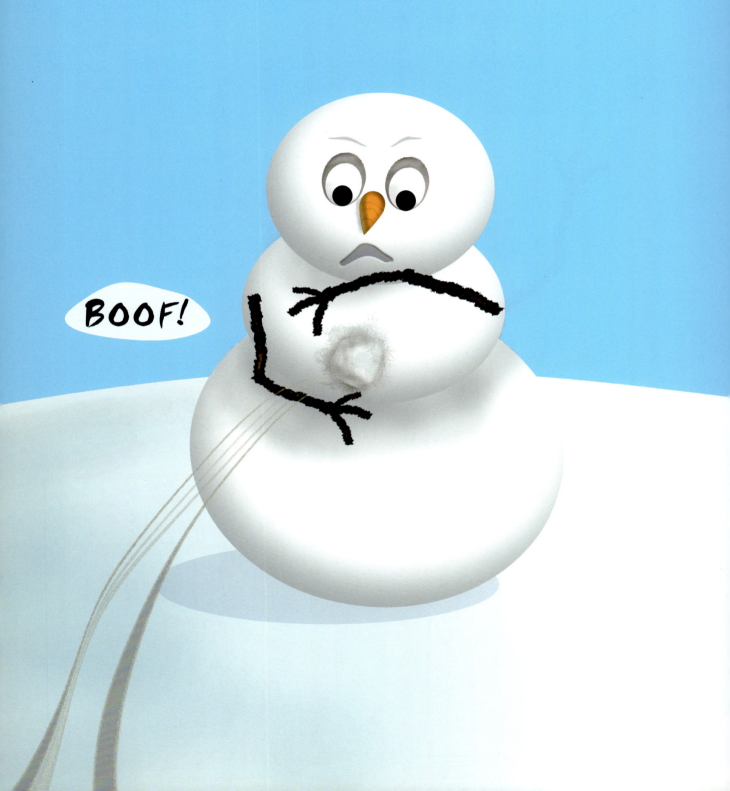

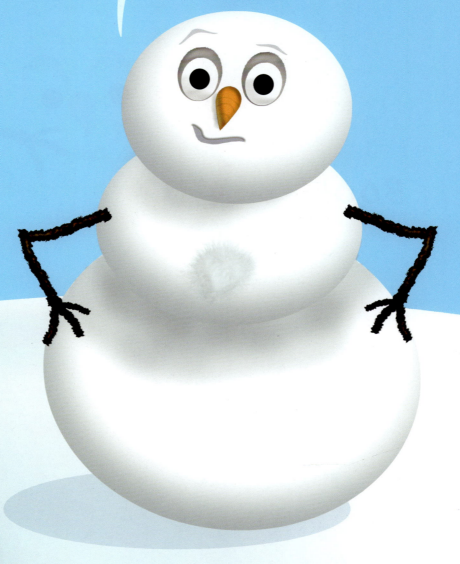

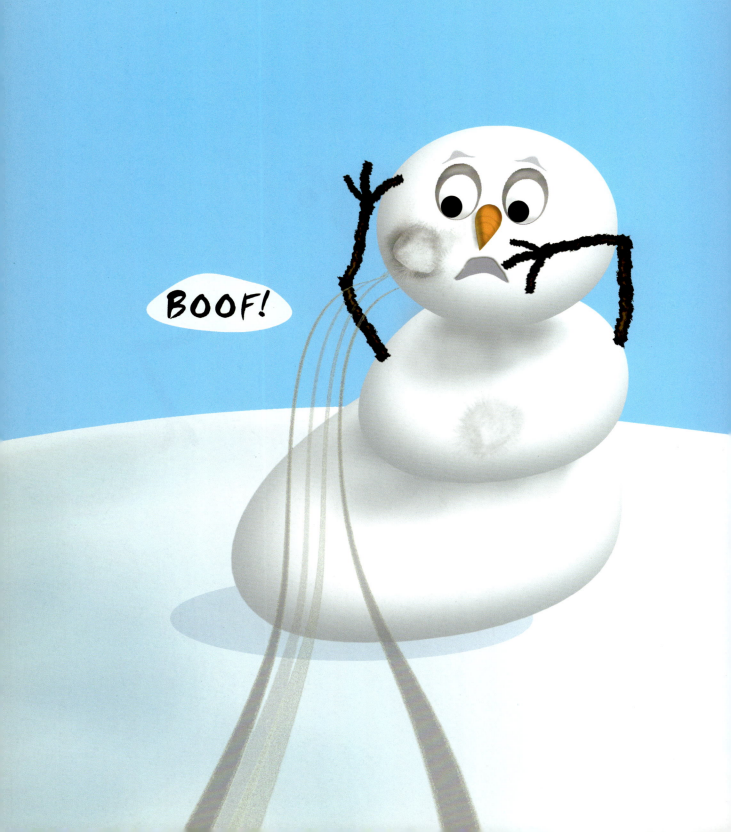

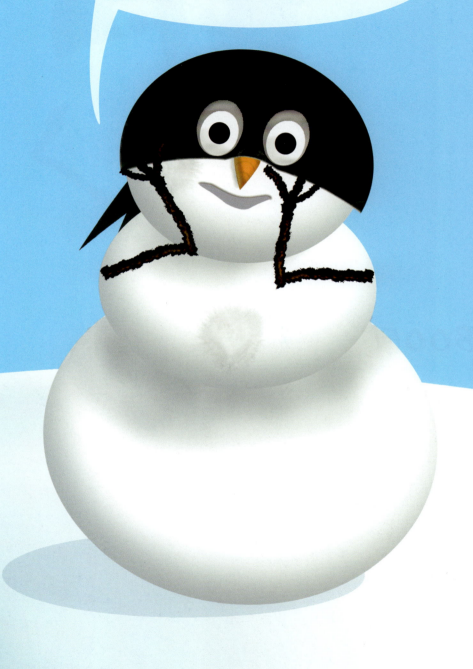

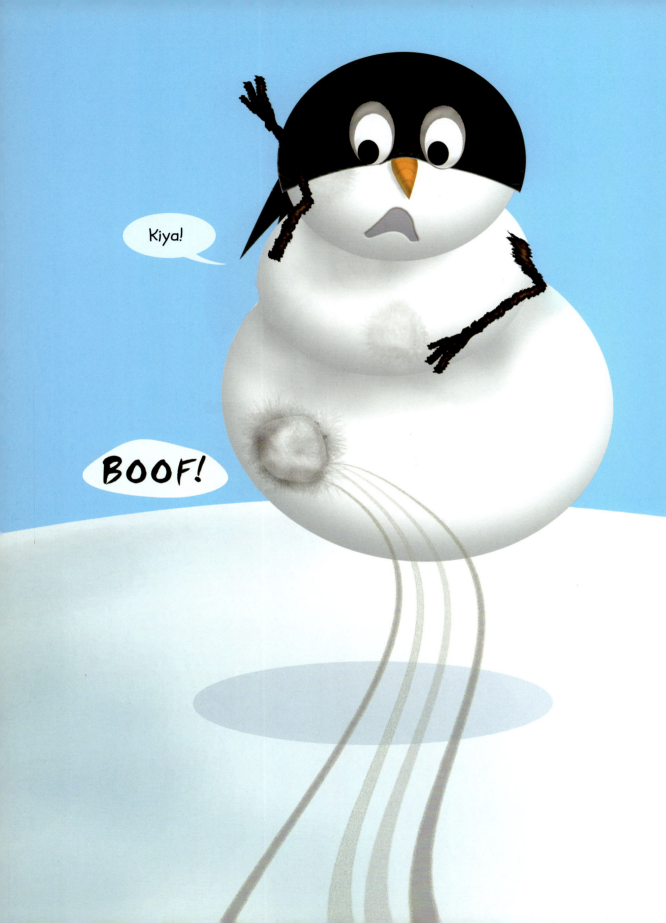

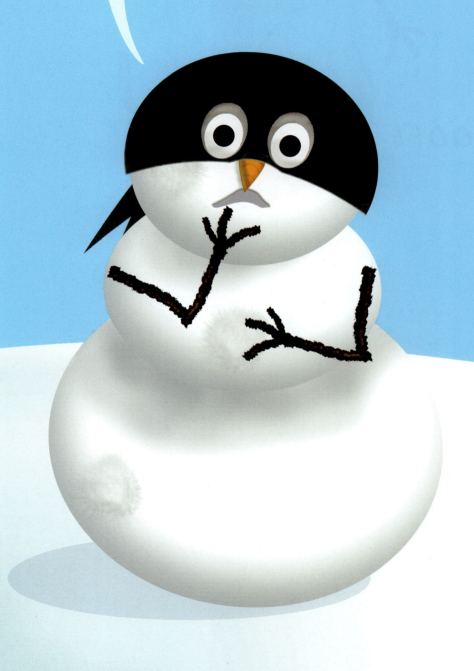

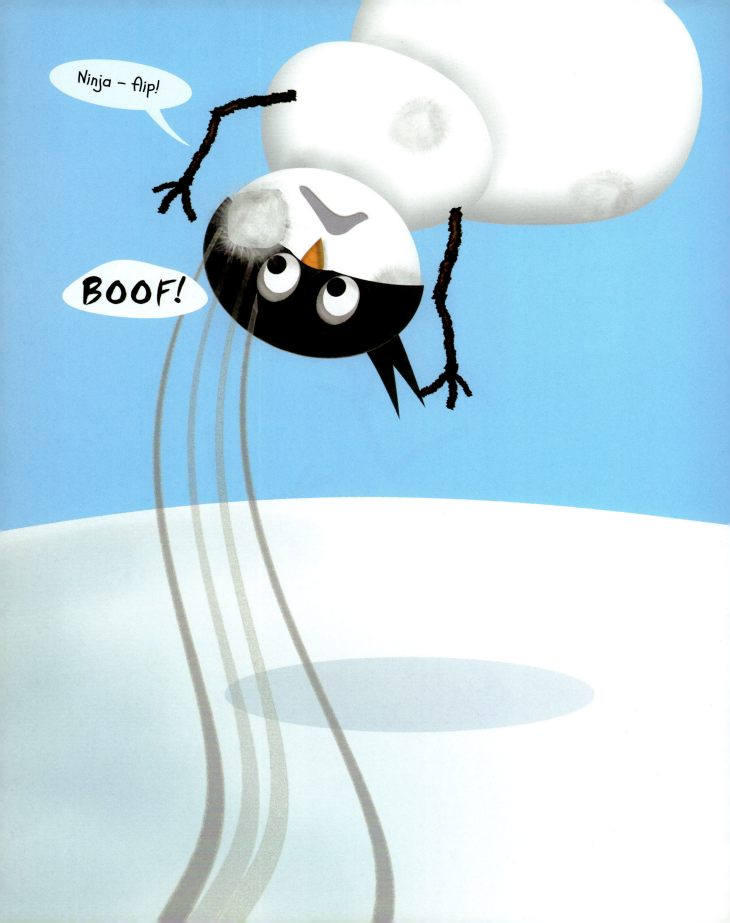

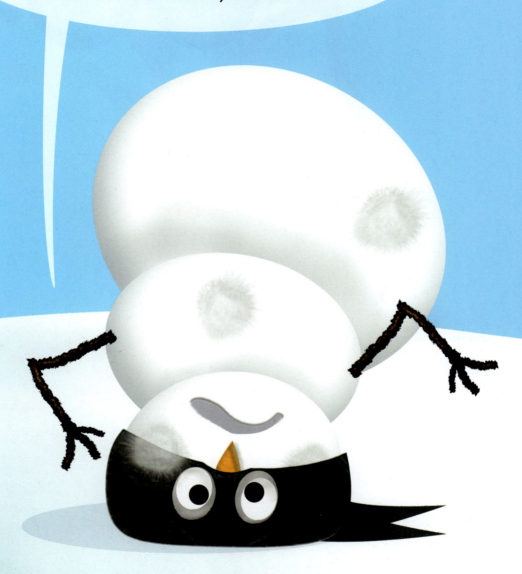

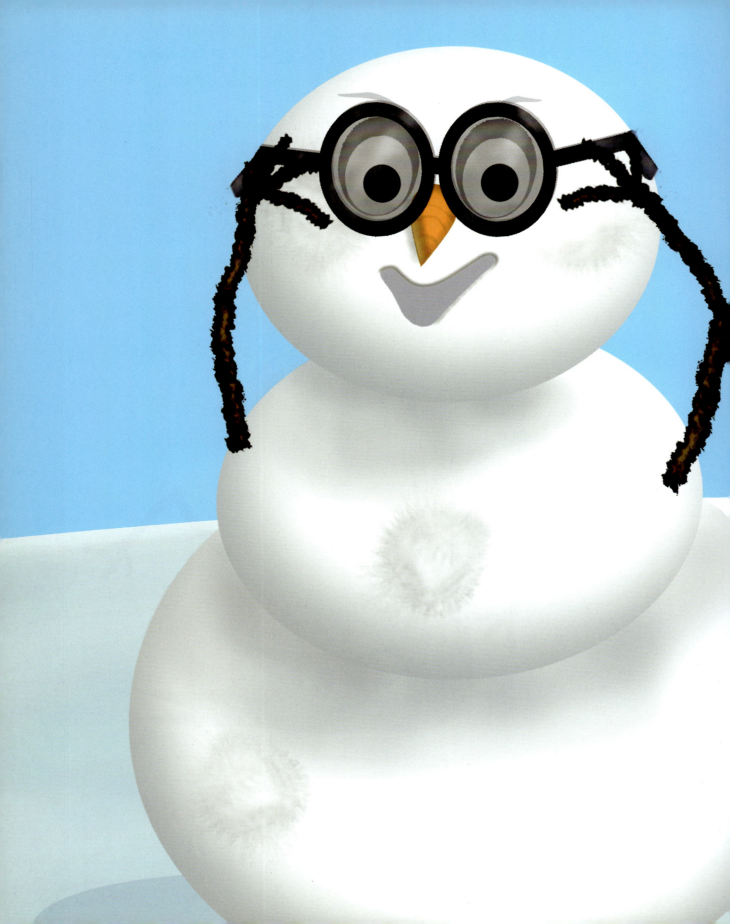

You wouldn't hit a snowman with glasses on, would you?
Go ahead. I dare you.

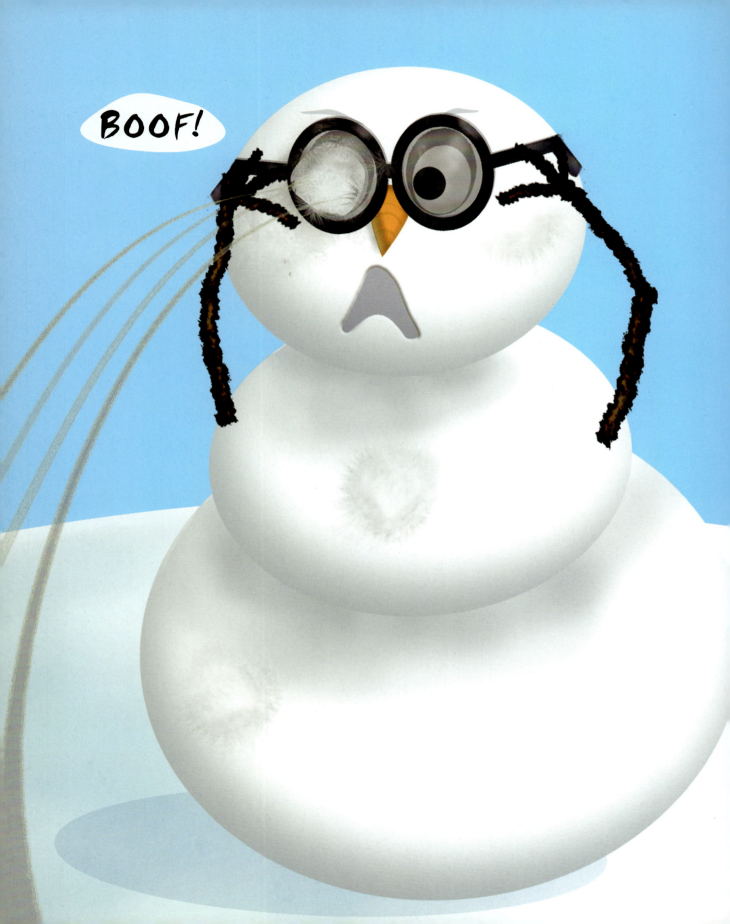

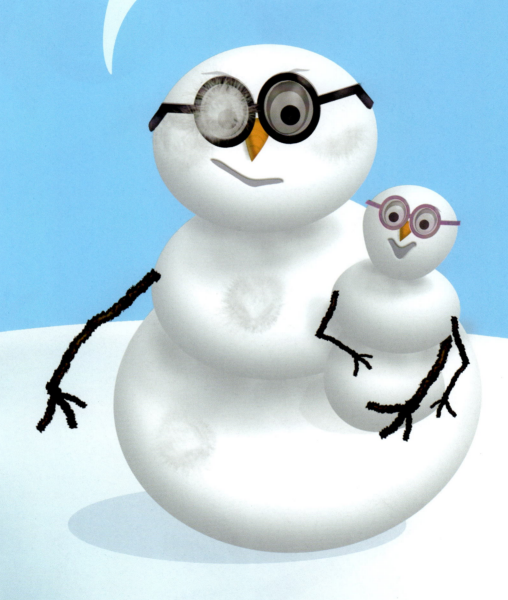

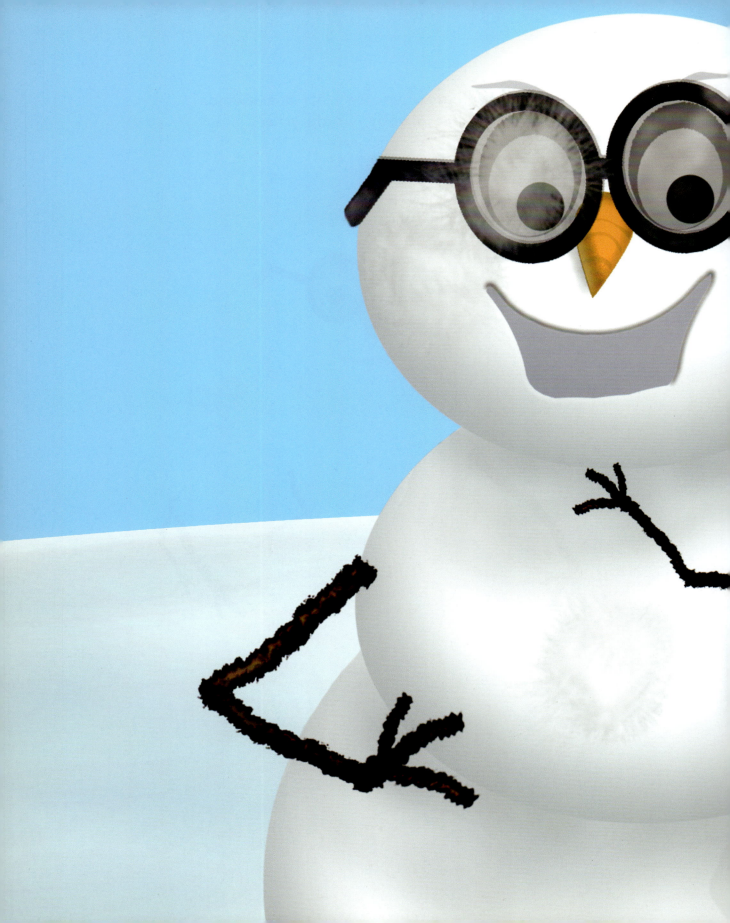

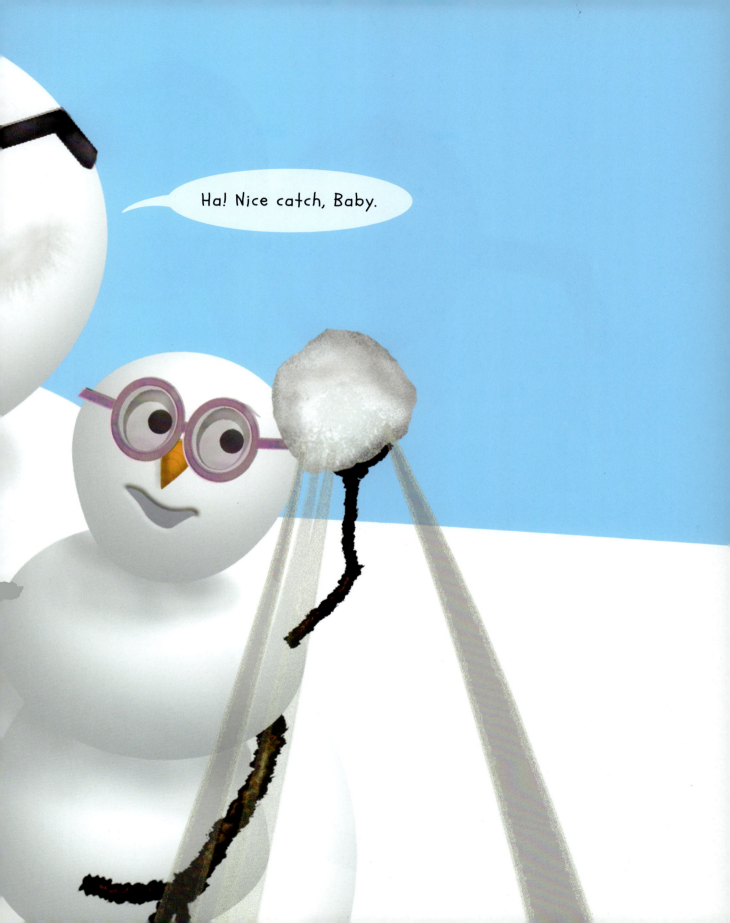

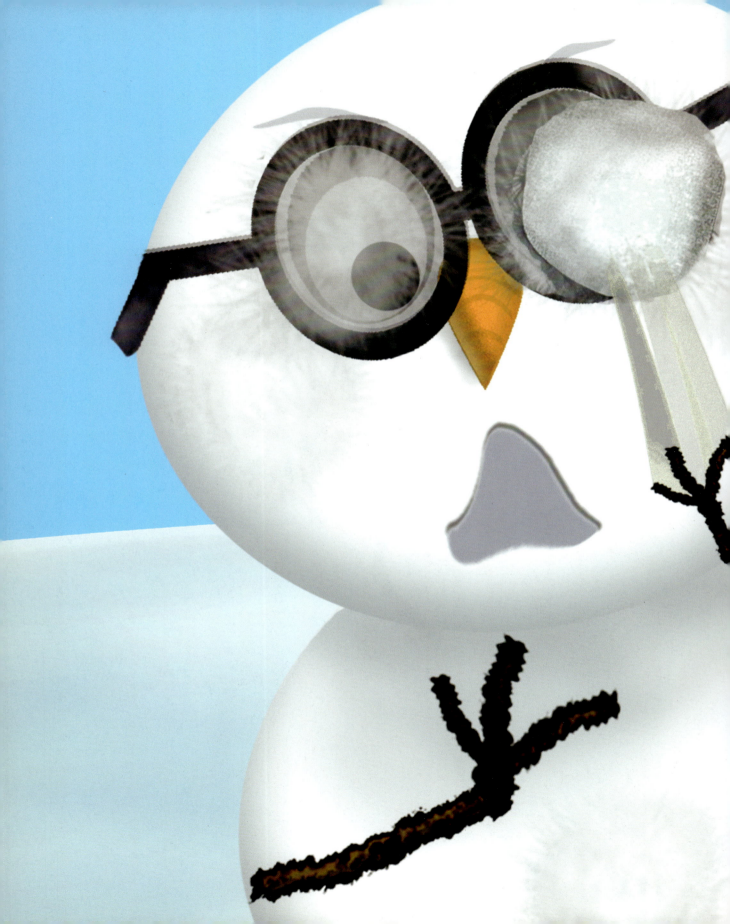

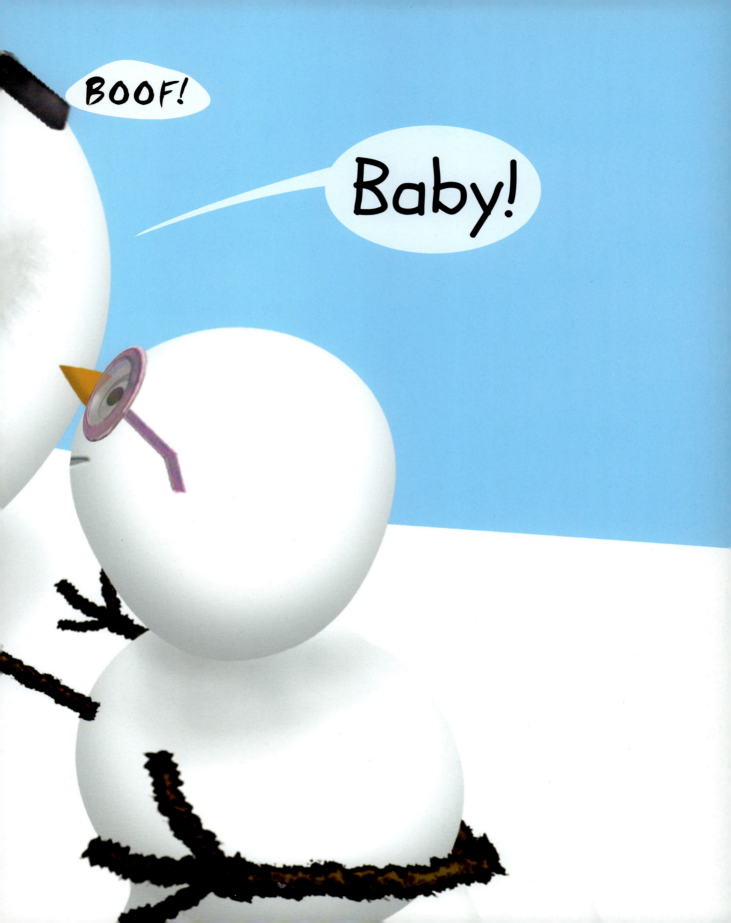

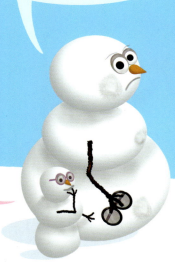

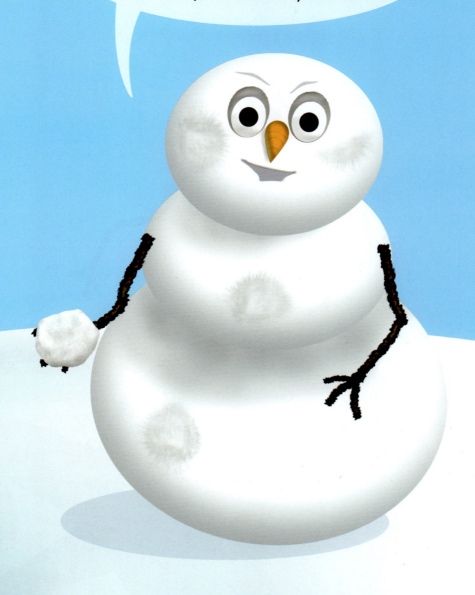

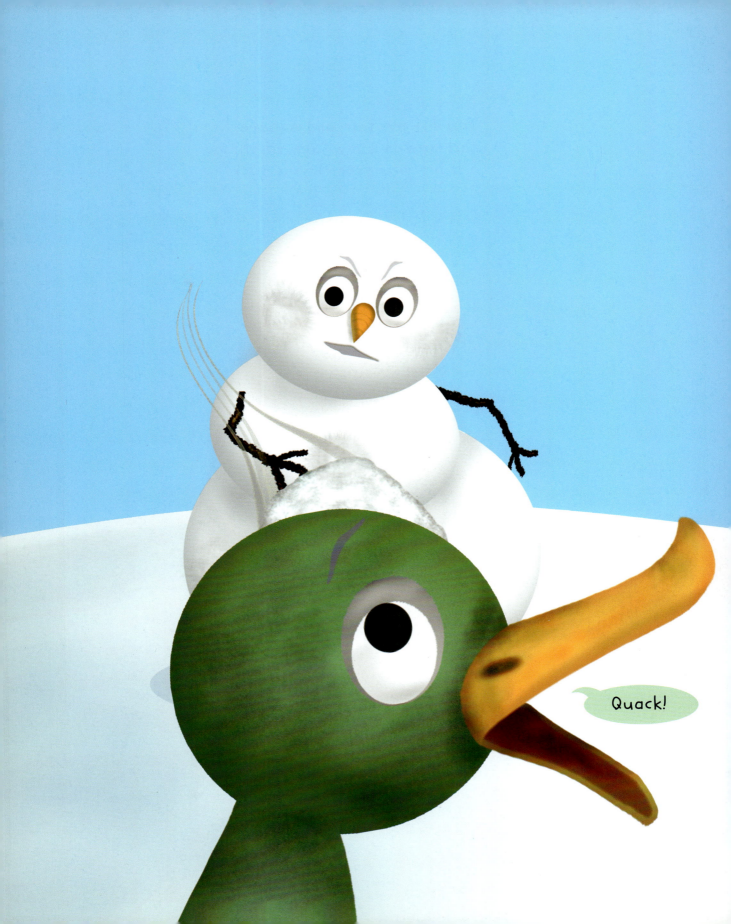

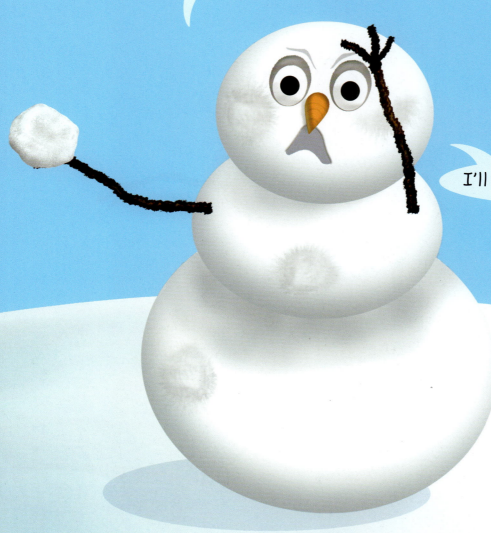

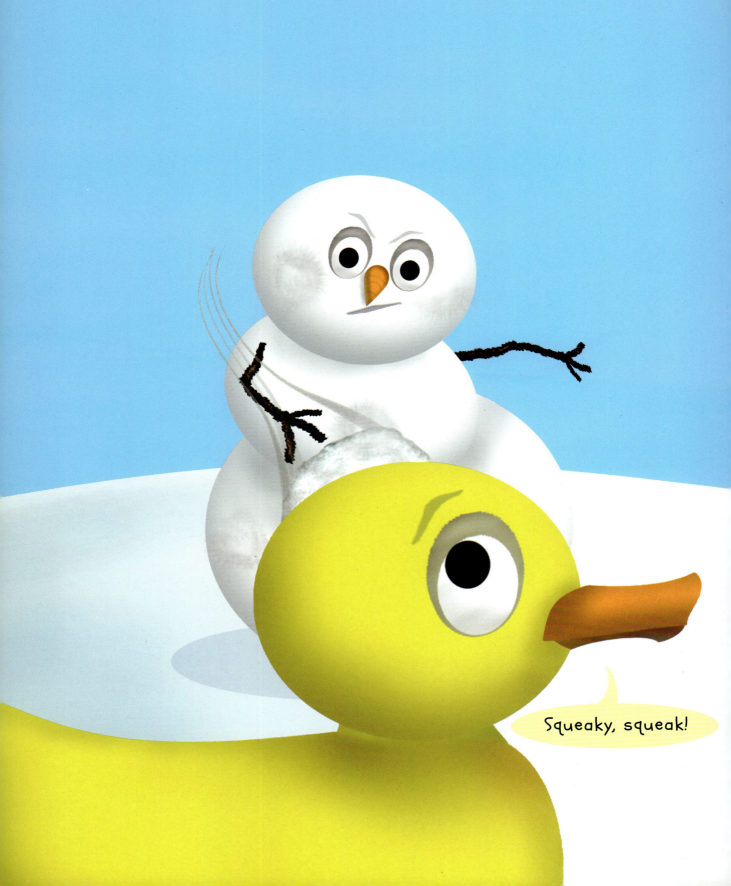

Not a rubber duck either!
This is ridiculous. I quit!

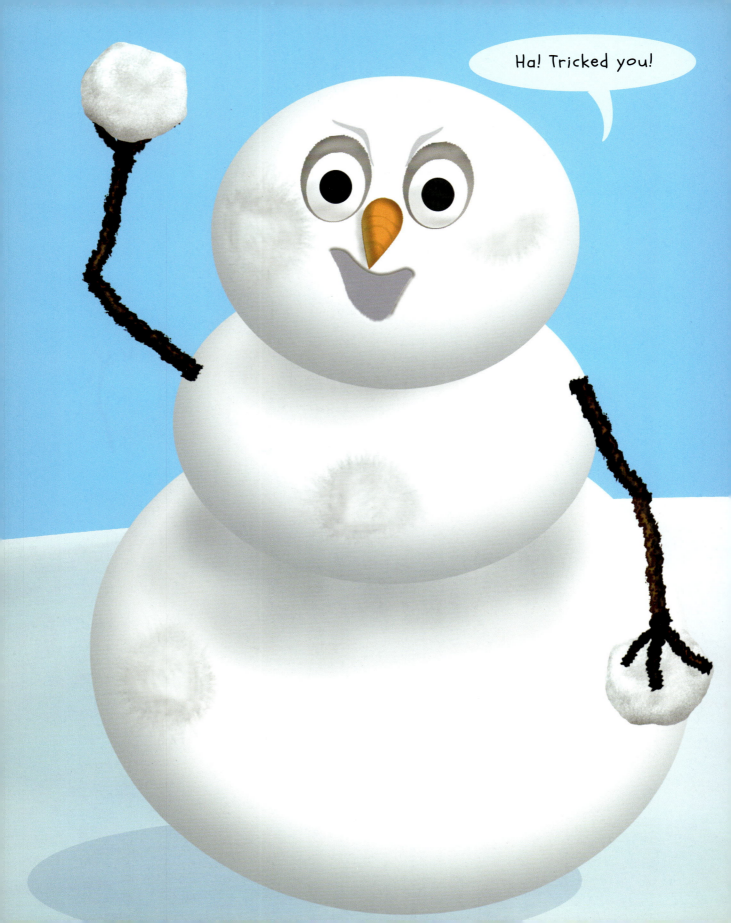

SNOWBALL FIGHT!

Throw! Throw! Throw! Throw! Throw!

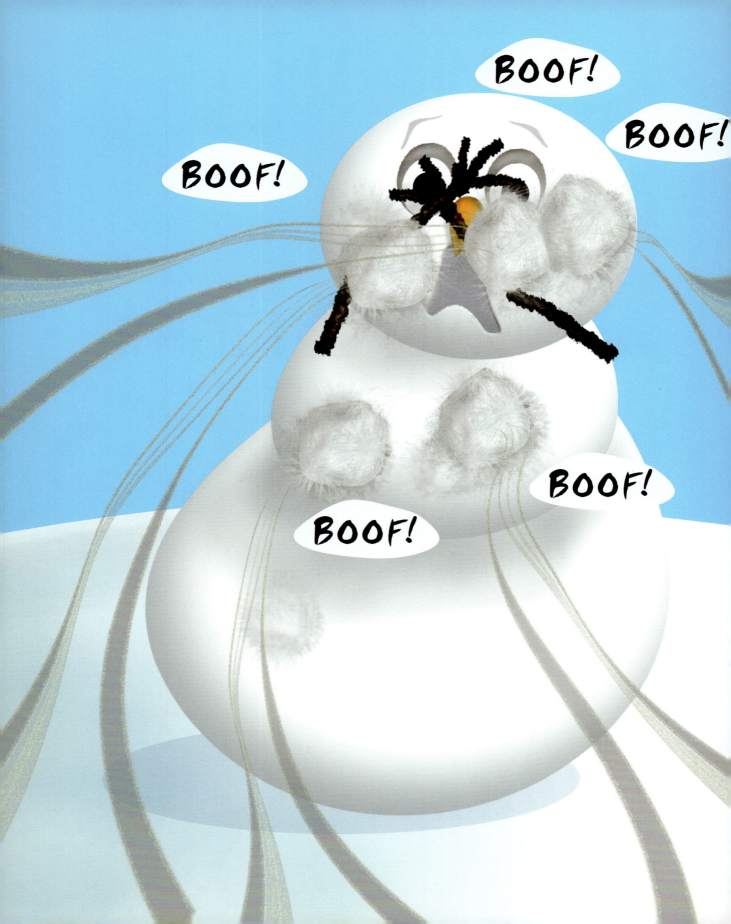

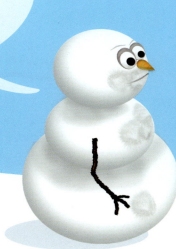

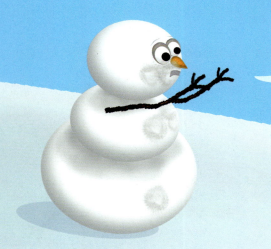

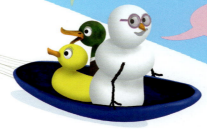

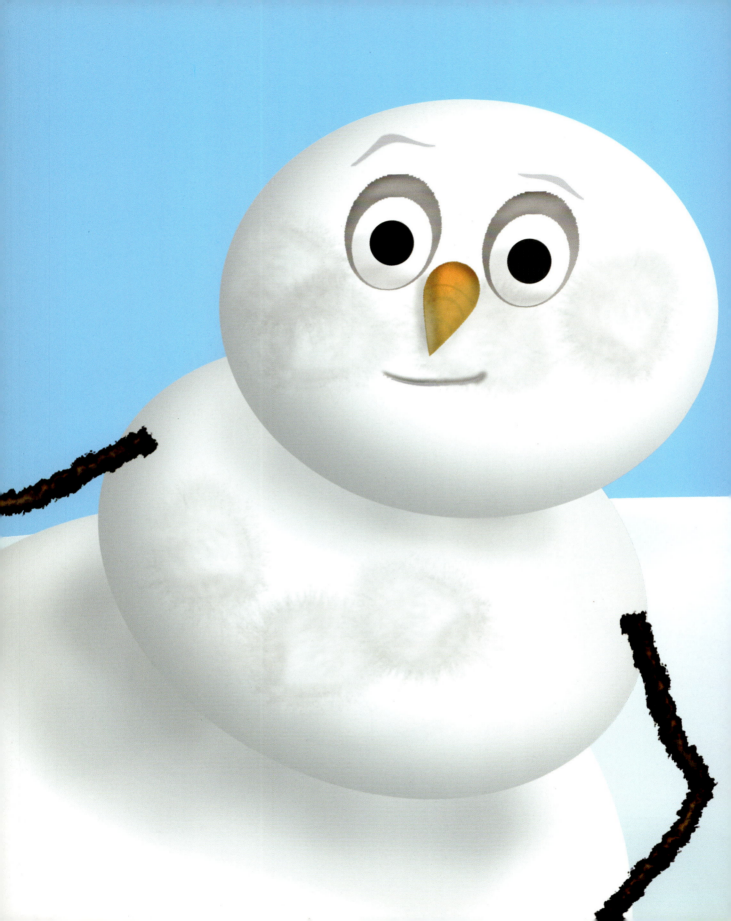

Reader, before you go.
Could you throw me a sled?
Please?

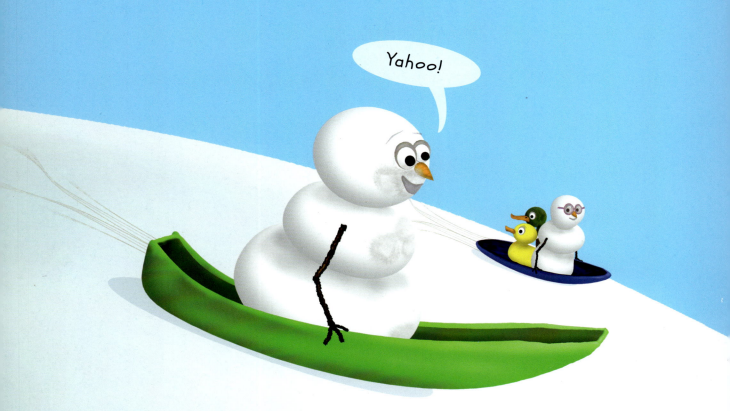